LEFT POLITICS AND THE LYRICS OF LYNYRD SKYNYRD: THE CONTRADICTION OF THE HUMAN EXPERIENCE EXAMINED THROUGH THE LENS OF POLITICAL ACTIVISM

(NEEDED: COVERT ART)

Copyright © 2025 Joseph Delia.

All rights reserved.

No part of this book may be reproduced, or stored in a retrieval system, or transmitted in any form or by any means, electronic, mechanical, photocopying, recording, or otherwise, without express written permission of the author.

ISBN: **979-8-9917187-3-8**

What you are holding in your hands is an invitation to a collaboration.

It is a book project I have been working on periodically since the mid to late 1980's.

This draft consists of 3 major sections.

1) An **Introduction** (that still needs to be expanded upon, as noted in the italicized second paragraph.)

2) A **Part One (or Chapter One)**, which just to be expanded upon, and then lead to potentially more chapters, etc.

3) A list of **5 Categories**, in which I have placed just some of the songs and lyrics of the band to reinforce the central thesis of the paper.

Please contact me if you have any comments, questions, ideas or, *more importantly, if you are willing to enter into a true collaborative effort to finish this project/book.*

I welcome any serious correspondence.

Joe Delia
July 2025
josephbdelia@gmail.com

CONTENTS

LEFT POLITICS AND THE LYRICS OF LYNYRD SKYNYRD	1
PART ONE (OR CHAPTER ONE)	7
CATEGORIES AND SONGS	9
ONE: THE MALE INDIVIDUALISTS' INTERACTION WITH WOMEN	11
TWO: THE SOUTHERN REACTION TO NORTHERN PREJUDICE	13
THREE: THE INDIVIDUALIST STRUGGLE AGAINST ORGANIZED SOCIETY	15
FOUR: RESPONSE TO MODERN CAPITALIST SOCIETY	17
FIVE: ALL KNOWLEDGE COMES FROM EXPERIENCE	19

LEFT POLITICS AND THE LYRICS OF LYNYRD SKYNYRD: THE CONTRADICTION OF THE HUMAN EXPERIENCE EXAMINED THROUGH THE LENS OF POLITICAL ACTIVISM

> Well, have you ever lived down in the Ghetto?
> Have you ever felt that cold wind blow?
> If you don't know what I mean,
> Why don't you stand up and scream,
> 'Cause there's things going on that you don't know.
> —-Ronnie Van Zant

Introduction

In the immediate aftermath of the 2004 election, the most widespread and compelling narrative coming from the political Left that spoke to the reasons for Bush's victory arguable came largely from one source. Thomas Frank's "What's the Matter with Kansas", appeared to offer a succinct, plausible explanation as to why so many working-class people voted for Bush against their economic self-interests. It traced the rise of the "Republican noise machine", with its roots in right-wing strategy sessions born out of the 1964 defeat of Barry Goldwater, and how it grew and expanded in the subsequent 40 years to become a powerful ideological weapon for Republican leaders and politicians in their quest to advance their overall conservative, pro-business agenda.

(Insert more on how this may be valuable for a larger scale analysis of how the discussion of "values" overtook economic interests in explaining the ideological success of the right-wing to frame the debate, it is important to delve deeper into the actual tension that exists in working-class people's world view, i.e., the contradictions that need to be highlighted and broken down, if we are to talk about theories or strategies that can push working-class people towards political action)

Joseph Delia

Although the premise of this project is to meld a progressive activism that is informed by the lyrics of a "rebel" 1970's rock band, my intention is for this book to have a popular circulation among activists involved in day-to-day radical politics. My motivation for embarking on this ostensibly unusual endeavor is to argue that a melding of people's culture and social theory is critical for all social activists studying working-class issues and who are seeking to articulate them in a way that advances those working-class interests. Also, I seek to start an initial dialogue between social activists and fans of the band. The common ground and organic alliance between these groups of people is one that I hope is made evident at the end of the book.

On the outset, the thought of any "alliance" or "common ground" between the typical progressive activist and the stereotypical Skynyrd listener (who may be perceived, albeit narrowly, as an apolitical male who drinks, smokes and shoots pool in a bar after a typical day of manual labor), may at first seem like a laughable anomaly. I recall a personal experience in the mid-1990's when I first started labor organizing and went on a house call to a worker's house with a young female organizer. In the rental car, I popped in a Skynyrd tape and after I began to sing along with it, my co-worker blurted out (as she turned down the volume), "How can you listen to that racist, red-neck music?" It was clear she saw no relation whatsoever between what she knew of my radical politics and my appreciation for Lynyrd Skynyrd; in fact, she saw them as contradictory.

Assuming that most people, in general, may not have such a harsh, immediate reaction to Skynyrd's music it was, nevertheless, a revealing comment. A comment that touches on the progressive communities' ignorance of and lack of appreciation of working-class experience and culture. Granted a comment like the one above, from a committed activist, might simply come from an ignorance of never really listening to the lyrics of the band and commits the classic ad homonym fallacy of logic: associating a style of music (southern music) with a stereotyped listener (that of a reactionary redneck). There is, however, a larger issue at play here.

Left Politics and the Lyrics of Lynyrd Skynyrd

There exists, in the progressive community, an inability to understand and even an unwillingness to relate to working class issues and experiences; critical issues that form not only the basis of Lynyrd Skynyrd's music but are crucial in the understanding and practice of working-class politics. Of course, one does not need to appreciate Skynyrds music in order to practice successful working-class politics. However, an appreciation and willingness to understand *the issues* the band wrote about will better prepare activists to carry out successful political action and strategy. In other words, to ignore and/or even downplay the themes and issues articulated in their music will necessarily result in a naive understanding of the working-class experience.

While it may be true that Skynyrd's music doesn't speak directly to the black-working class experience or any other minority experiences in this country, to say it only represents the experiences of southern white males, would be wrong. Although the music was born in a specific region of the country and reflects a 1970's environment their music does reflect many themes that are common to all working-class people, regardless of race, creed or sex.

These common themes, then, those of struggling to make ends meet; the hardships of working day in and day out for a living; the trials and tribulations of personal relationships; the struggle for individual freedom and identity; the respect and appreciation for elders, and the centrality of family, community and God in one's life are not only themes that run throughout the music of Skynyrd but are also central issues that are important to the working-class communities of today.

At this point one might ask "Why Lynyrd Skynyrd?... Why not some other band?" That question can be answered quite simply. Skynyrd's brand of music and honest, working-class lyrics make the band the hands down candidate for this type of analysis and integration with political theory. On a purely objective scale, no other band with world-wide stature and long-lasting staying power has appeared on the scene with such a consistent and all-encompassing working-class background inherent to its lyrics and style of music than Skynyrd.

This "world-wide stature" component is a critical factor in the decision to concentrate on Lynyrd Skynyrd in particular. To argue for the integration of just *any* band's ideology would be an exercise in ill-relevance. No doubt there are smaller, less popular bands and artists that articulate a sharper political and sophisticated working-class message, but they never are or were as big as Skynyrd[1]. The issue here is bridging the gap between realms of *mass appeal*: the realm of rock music with its world-wide exposure and the (potentially large) realm of mass social activism.

Ronnie Van Zant, co-founder and chief lyricist of the original band, once said that Lynyrd Skynyrd was "just street people", trying to write "common songs for the common people."[2] An examination of the roots of the band members as well as the songs they produced, bear witness to that statement. The core members of the band were raised in a working-class neighborhood on the west side of Jacksonville, Florida, dropped out of school at 16 years old and devoted their lives full-time to their music. Van Zant described his old neighborhood as "rough… particularly where I grew up. It was like a ghetto, black and white, and there was a lot of street fighting."[3] In many respects they were no different from most bands that started out in the South during the late 1960's; they were influenced by black delta music, Rhythm and Blues, the "British invasion" and of course, traditional country music. It was this fusion of all the above that would lead to their unique sound and ultimately their immense popularity.

The musical themes and lyrics of the band reflect the members' upbringing, values, and commonality with all people who work for a living. In many ways their music was intensely personal; in fact, one gets a sense of the issues and struggles that the band was coping with at any given stage in their career from their song choices they put on

---

[1] One could certainly argue that Billy Bragg, for example, might exhibit a more sophisticated working-class message in his music than is evident in Skynyrds. However, it is generally calculated that Skynyrd's MCA catalogue has sold in excess of 30 million albums, compared to Billy Bragg's _____ need #.

[2] Quoted in "American by Birth" by Ron O' in Brien with Andy McKaie, liner notes, *Lynyrd Skynyrd Anthology*, MCA, p.4.

[3] "Lynyrd Skynyrd in Turmoil. "By Scott Cohen. *Circus Raves New York*, Sept. 1975, pp. 26-30.

each of their successive albums. In other words, most all their music was written specifically about the intense personal changes and inner conflicts they experienced during their meteoric rise from poor working-class musicians to world-touring rock-n-roll superstars. This is not unusual, in that most bands and songwriters are influenced by changes throughout their own lives and careers; however, there was a continuity in the music of Lynyrd Skynyrd that reflected an honesty, an integrity and an affirmation of their working-class roots that *was never lost* throughout their short but prolific career.[4]

While the themes, issues and concerns they sang about in the 1970's are still reflective of similar themes, issues and concerns found in working-class communities of today, this book will largely focus on a bigger issue: The contradiction within the human condition.

> *(Need to expand this paragraph more and reinforce the central thesis of the book).*

Also included is a brief survey of just a sample of the lyrics of the band, placed into 5 categories, that explore seemingly conflicting themes and attitudes expressed throughout their music.

A note to the reader is warranted here. This is a purely *theoretical* book. In other words, I will not attempt to offer any political action plan or strategy. I will leave that to others to develop a *practice*. It is my hope that the theoretical threads found inside these pages might lead to a practical and concrete political strategy that informs our current politics. *Especially* since the emergence and consolidation of fascism that began in the United States around 2016, and continues to grow in various parts of the world.

---

[4] **IMPORTANT NOTE: This paper will only deal with the *original* band line up before the plane crash of 1977 which killed, among others, Ronnie Van Zandt, co-founder and chief lyricist for the band. This would include all five studio albums (1973-1977) and the various recordings and session work that was done with Van Zandt.**

Joseph Delia

PART ONE (OR CHAPTER ONE)

> *"Human beings are tissues of contradictions, and the life even of the intellectual is not logic, to borrow from Holmes, but experience."* [5]

When one surveys the totality of the lyrics of Skynyrd found on their first five studio albums, one is struck by the seemingly contradictory viewpoints of their attitudes and politics towards life in general. At first glance, their "back and forth" views on personal relationships, drug use, politics and community, might leave one with the impression that there is no consistency to their orientation and politics on these various topics.

In fact, depending on the song one picks, one's first impression of the band might be that they are nothing more than a bunch of provincial, drug induced hell raisers who have little regard for women and engage in individualist and paranoid thinking. On the other hand, looking at another set of songs one might hear a voice shaped by wisdom and old age experience that belies the life experience of kids in their early twenties and, further, shows a maturity and cogent understanding of their environment and U.S. society at large.

It is only, then, through an examination of their complete lyrical catalogue that one can envisage a "holistic" worldview at play; holistic in the sense that it represents a wide range of contradictions that inform the very nature of the human condition. *Why* this is important should be apparent in the current technological age we are living. As David Runciman suggests in his book *The Handover*:

> *We are going to be living in a world of human-like machines, built by machine like versions of human beings. To fixate on the human would be a mistake, because the merely human will be relatively powerless to impact on this future. It's not a question of us versus them. It's a question of which of them gives us the best chance of being us.* [6]

---

[5] "Anti-Intellectualism in American Life", by Richard Hofstadler, Vintage Books, 1962, p. 32.
[6] "The Handover: How We Gave Control of Our Lives to Corporations, States and AIs", by David Runciman, Liveright Publishing Corporation, 2023, (paperback edition, 2024), p. 10.

Joseph Delia

CATEGORIES AND SONGS

Skynyrds' songs can be categorized in a variety of ways. For the sake of this book, I have attempted to group just a handful of their songs into five separate categories.

1. **The Male Individualists Interaction with Women**
2. **The Southern Reaction to Northern Prejudice**
3. **The Individualists Struggle against Organized Society**
4. **Response to Modern Capitalist Society**
5. **All Knowledge Comes from Experience**

After each song, I have included a few lines which I feel best captures the important kernel of the song's "essence", if you will.

Note: It should go without saying, that the distinctive male "voice" expressed *in all these songs* can easily be swapped out for any other "voice", depending on the reader's gender or sexual orientation.

Joseph Delia

ONE

The Male Individualists' Interaction with Women

I Know a Little

...I don't know where you've been last night, but I'm thinking mama you ain't doing right...

Trust

...don't tell your women that you love her, 'cause that's when your trouble begins...

On The Hunt

...I said Babe, mama I don't know your name... I said Babe, sugar I can play your game...

One More Time

...yes, I'm her fool once more, I can read her brown eyes... when the rooster crows tomorrow, well it's her turn to cry...

Cheatin' Woman

...A cheatin' woman will make you crazy, a cheatin' woman will make you a fool...you love any man with pants on... seems like nothing pleases you...

Gimme Three Steps

...wait a minute mister, I didn't even kiss her, don't want no trouble with you...

Tuesday's Gone

...Tuesday, you see, she had to be free... somehow, I've got to carry on...

I Ain't the One

...You talkin' jive, woman, when you say to me, that your daddy's goin' to take us in, mama, take care of me...

Made In the Shade

>...when I look at look at your face, baby, when I look into your eyes, I can tell pretty mama, I've been wastin' time... 'cause you don't love really love me...

Free Bird

>...we'll I must be traveling on now, 'cause there's too many places I've got to see...

I've Never Dreamed

>...I never dreamed that it could feel so good, Lord, that two could be one...

TWO

The Southern Reaction to Northern Prejudice

Swamp Music

...Go ahead... just take that city hike...well, I'd rather live with the hound dogs for the rest of my natural born life...

All I Can Do Is Write About It in A Song

...well, I can see the concrete slowing creepin', Lord take me and mine before they come... you can take a boy out of ol' Dixie land, but you'll never take ol' Dixie from a boy...

Mississippi Kid

...well, I was born in Mississippi, and I don't take any stuff from you...

Comin' Home

...concrete jungle surrounded me, many nights I've slept out in the streets... paid my dues and I've changed my style, I've seen hard times over now...

Sweet Home Alabama

...I heard ole' Neil put her down... I hope Neil Young will remember... southern man doesn't need him around anyhow...

Down South Jukin

...and do some down South Jukin, lookin' for a piece of mind...

I'm a Country Boy

...New York City is a thousand miles away, and if you ask me that's ok by me...I'm not trying to put the big apple down, but they don't need men like me in town...

Joseph Delia

THREE

The Individualist Struggle Against Organized Society

Double Trouble

...I was born down in the gutter, with a temper as hot as fire... some of the time I was innocent, but the judge said 'guilty'...

Don't Ask Me No Questions (and I Won't Tell You No Lies)

...when I get home, nobody wants to let me be...don't you think that when I come home, I just wanna have my time...

Whiskey Rock-n-Roller

...sometimes I wonder, where will we go, Lord, don't you take my, whiskey Rock-n-Roll...

White Dove

...tired of fighting, wanna lay down my gun...just wanna know that my work is done...

One In the Sun

...somewhere there's people laughing...they think they've found a way... but it's not me, no, no... I'm not the one in the sun...

Roll Gypsy Roll

...10 years on this road is bound to take its toll...

Wino

...guess he's a happy young man, God in heaven only knows...

Call Me The Breeze (written by J.J.Cale)

...I ain't hiding from nobody, nobody hiding from me... and that's the way it's supposed to be...

Joseph Delia

FOUR

Response to Modern Capitalist Society

Saturday Night Special

...handguns were made for killin', ain't no good for nothing else... so why don't we dump 'em, people...to the bottom of the sea, before some ol' fool come around here and wanna shoot either you or me...

Things Goin' On

...too much money they spend across the ocean, too much money they spend on the moon... until they make things right, I hope they never sleep at night, they better make some changes through here soon...

That Smell

...Angle of darkness is upon you, can't speak a word when your full up with ludes...

Mr. Banker

...Mr. Banker...how much does money mean? ... won't you reconsider mister; won't you bury my papa for me...

Ain't No Good Life

...just cause I'm alive, that don't mean I'm making a living... well I can't make any money baby, cause my money is already spent...and I know where it went, it went on that damn rent...

Four Walls of Raiford

...well now they say I'm guilty, when they find me, I must die... only me and Jesus know that I never stole a dime...

Lend a Helping Hand

...if you've ever seen the tortured eyes from a foreign land... if you've ever felt the pain inside, I know you'd understand...

Joseph Delia

FIVE

All Knowledge Comes from Experience

Simple Man

...Mama told me, when I was young... forget your lust for the rich man's gold. All that you need is in your soul...

Searching

...you got stacks of money to the sky up above, now all you need is to find you a love...

Ballad of Curtis Lowe

...Ole' Curt was black man, with white curly hair.... people said he was useless, them people all were fools, 'cause Curtis Lowe was the finest picker to ever play the blues...

Am I Losin'

...now my friend won't talk to me, let me tell you why... he thinks I've changed because of the dollar sign...why won't my friend take me as I am, because your friend is the most important thing...

He's Alive

...but now you are gone, and I'm on my own...but I realized one thing, one man is never alone...

Cry For the Bad Man

... he knocked me down, now I'm on my feets... and now I'm so much wiser...

Truck Drivin' Man

...well, I'm talkin' about, the truck drivin' man... yes, he'll always give you the best that he can...

Joseph Delia

Poison Whiskey

...take a tip from me, brothers can't you see, ...ain't no future in ol' poison whiskey... the doctor just shook his head, the only thing he's gonna tell you is to stop drinking Johnny Walker's Red... twenty years of rot gut whisky done kill that poor man dead...

www.ingramcontent.com/pod-product-compliance
Lightning Source LLC
Chambersburg PA
CBHW020450030426
42337CB00014B/1481